Dot Markers Activity Book

Happy Easter

Ages 2+

With BIG DOT Circles

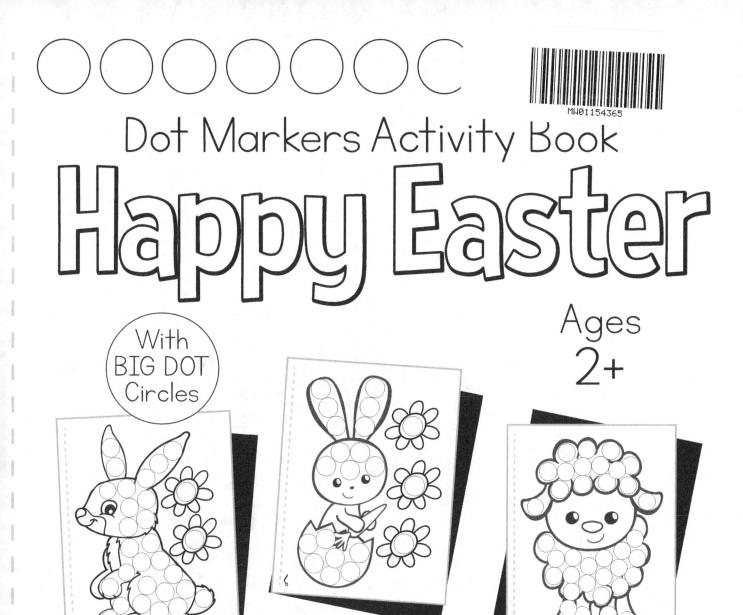

This book is made to be used with paint daubers or dot markers. Each page has a black background on the reverse to help with bleed-through. Also, you can cut out each page using the trim line or use a separate piece of paper between pages. Have fun!

This book belongs to:

_____

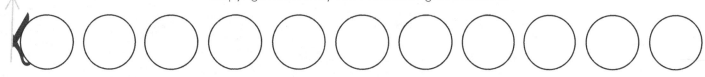

Let's practice with dot markers!

Let's practice with dot markers!

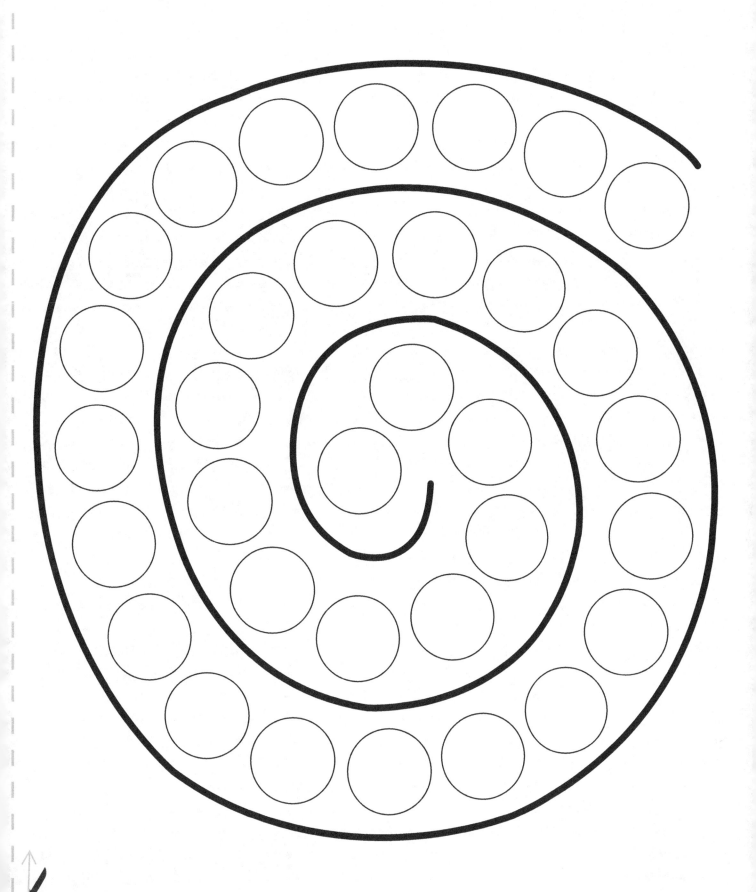

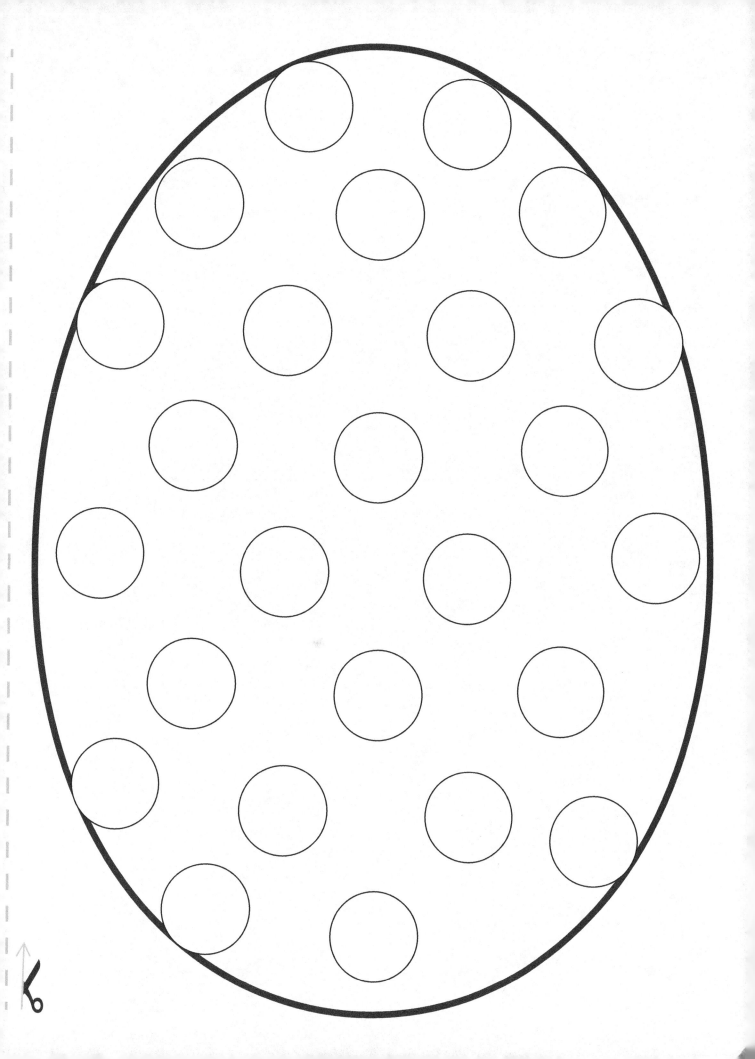

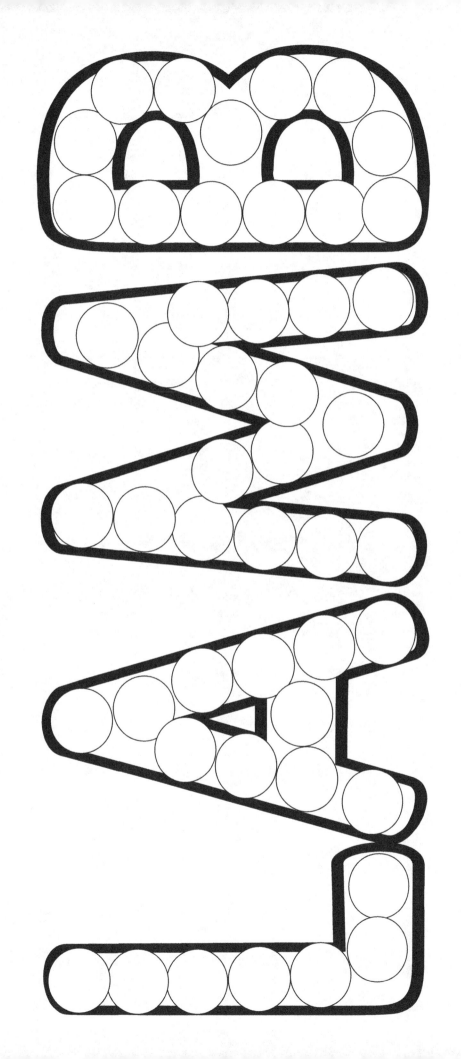

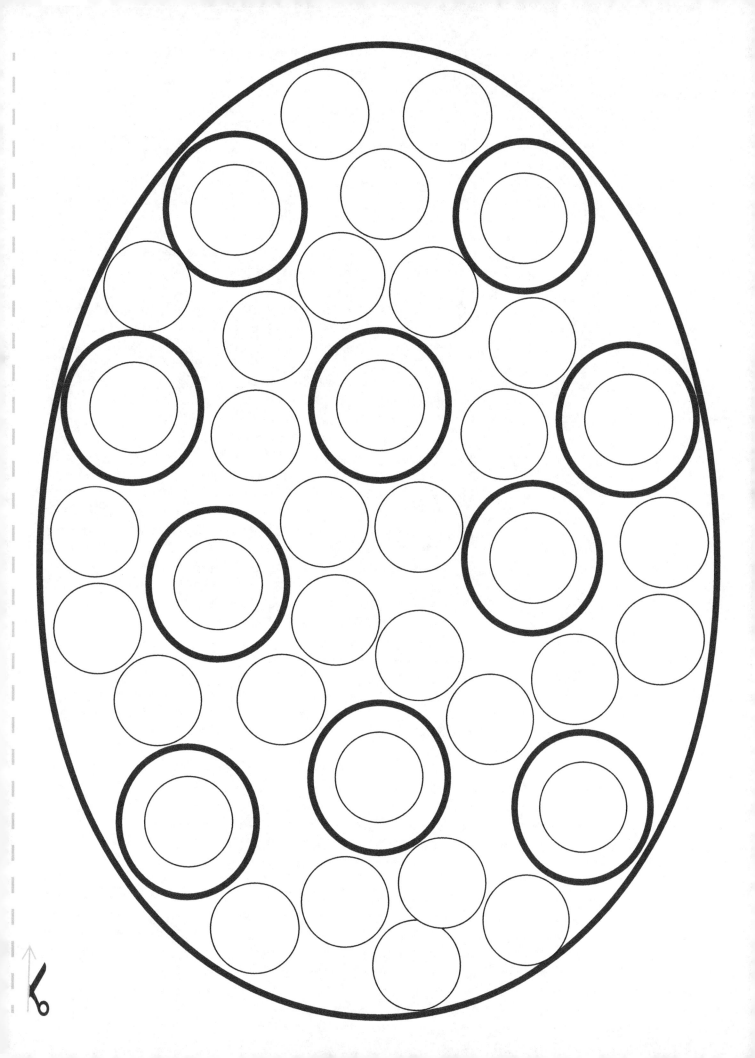

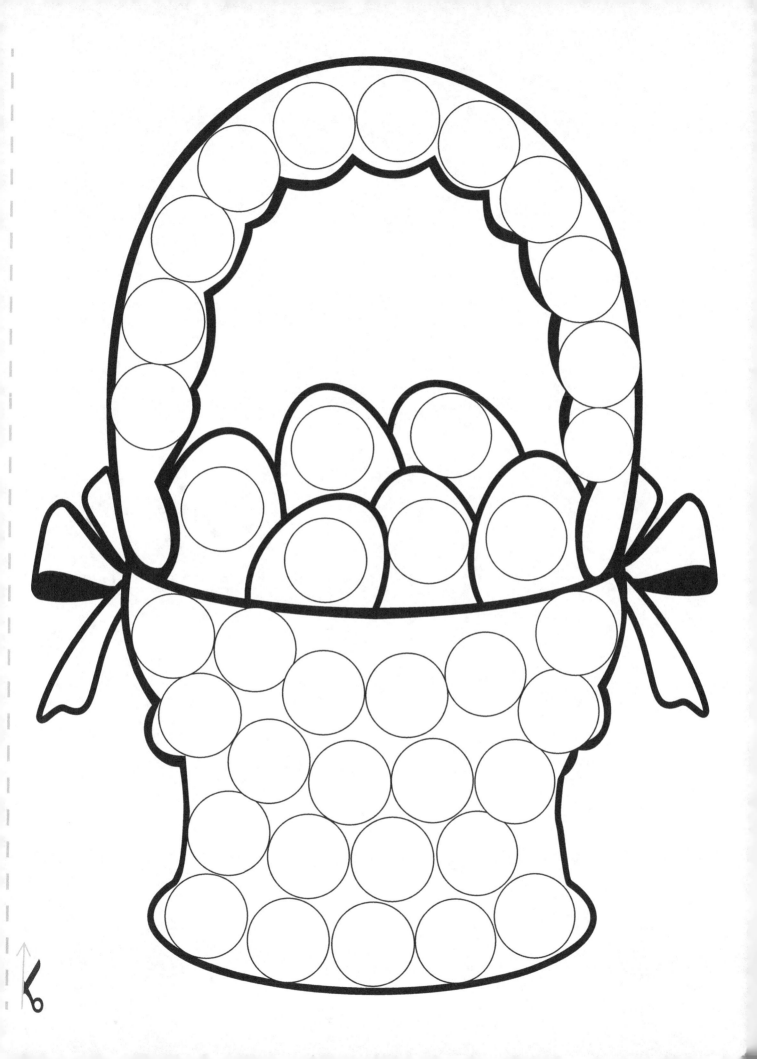

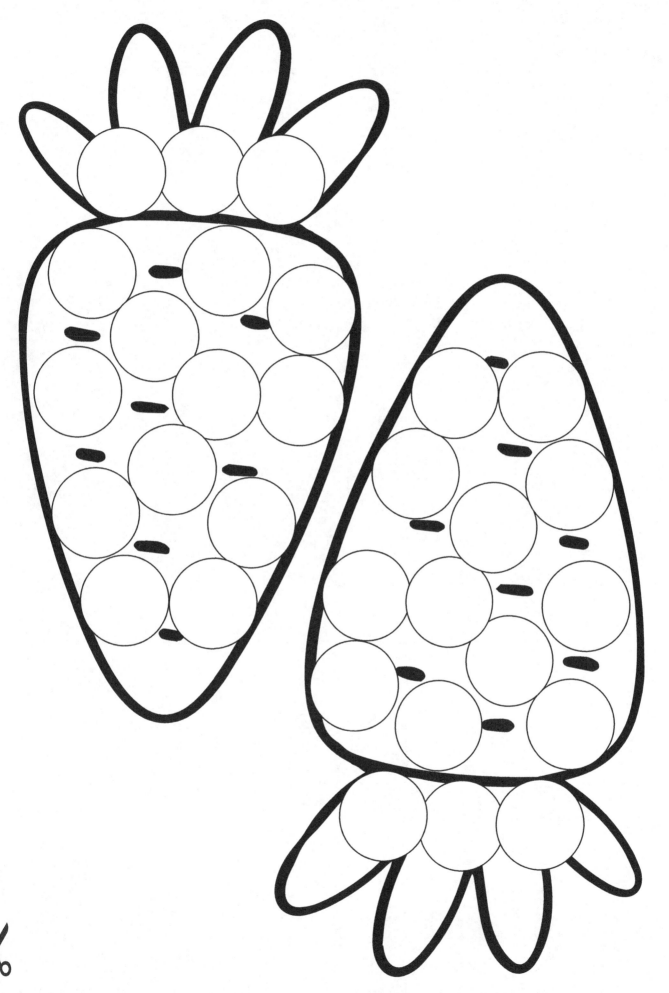

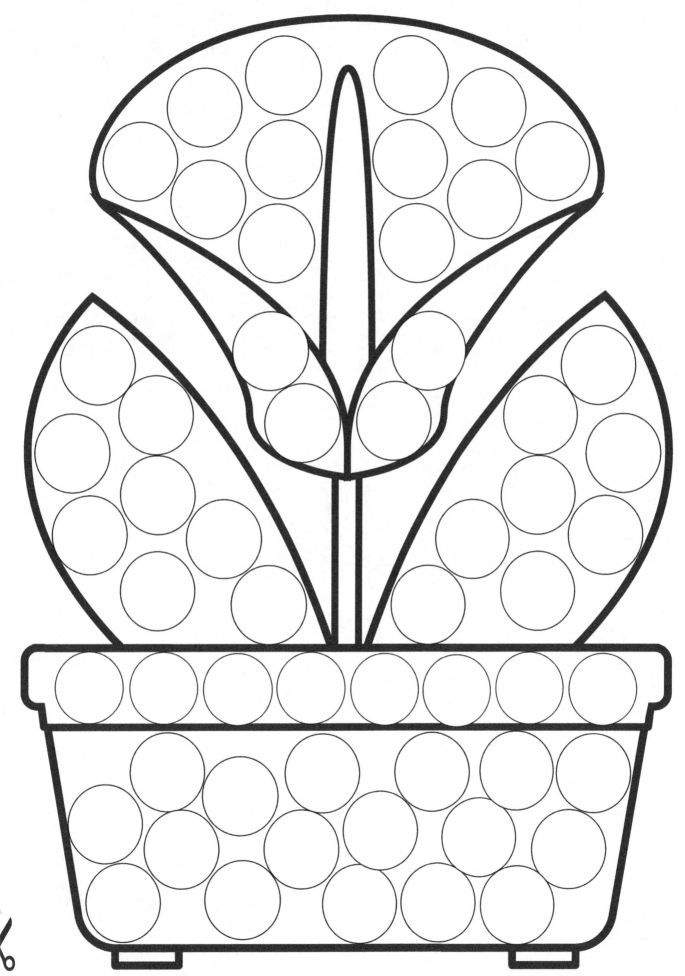

Made in the USA
Las Vegas, NV
25 February 2024

86312640R00044